A BOOK OF WITNESS

D0558097

Also by Jerome Rothenberg

POEMS

White Sun Black Sun (1960)
Between: Poems 1960-1963 (1967)
Poems 1964-1967 (1968)
Poems for the Game of Silence (1971)
Poland/1931 (1974)
A Seneca Journal (1978)
Vienna Blood (1980)
That Dada Strain (1983)
New Selected Poems 1970-1985 (1986)
Khurbn & Other Poems (1989)
The Lorca Variations (1993)
Gematria (1993)
Seedings & Other Poems (1996)
A Paradise of Poets (1999)

TRANSLATIONS

New Young German Poets (1959)
Hochhuth's "The Deputy," playing version (1965)
Enzensberger's "Poems for People Who Don't Read Poems," with Michael Hamburger (1968)
The Book of Hours & Constellations, or Gomringer by Rothenberg (1968)
The 17 Horse Songs of Frank Mitchell X-XIII (1973)
15 Flower World Variations (1984)
Schwitters' "Poems Performance Pieces Proses Plays Poetics (PPPPPP)," with Pierre Joris (1993)
Lorca's "Suites" (2001)
Nezval's "Antilyrik & Other Poems," with Milos Sovak (2001)
Picasso's "The Burial of Count Orgaz & Other Poems," with Pierre Joris (2003)

ANTHOLOGIES

Technicians of the Sacred (1968, 1985)
Shaking the Pumpkin (1972, 1986)
America a Prophecy, with George Quasha (1973)
Revolution of the Word (1974)
A Big Jewish Book, with Harris Lenowitz and Charles Doria (1977)
Symposium of the Whole, with Diane Rothenberg (1983)
Exiled in the Word, with Harris Lenowitz (1989)
Poems for the Millennium (2 vols.), with Pierre Joris (1995 and 1998)
A Book of the Book, with Steven Clay (2000)

RECORDINGS

From a Shaman's Notebook (1968)
Origins & Meanings (1968)
Horse Songs & Other Soundings (1975)
6 Horse Songs for 4 Voices (1978)
Signature, with Charles Morrow (2002)

PROSE

Pre-Faces & Other Writings (1981)
The Riverside Interviews (1984)

A BOOK OF WITNESS
Spells & Gris-Gris

JEROME ROTHENBERG

A NEW DIRECTIONS BOOK

ACKNOWLEDGMENTS

Some of these poems first appeared in the following editions by Jerome Rothenberg: *Un Cruel Nirvana: Poemas 1980-2000* (Tucán de Virginia, México, 2001); *The Case for Memory* (Ian Tyson & Granary Books, France & New York, 2001); *Livre de Témoignage,* with art by Arman (Editions Tiar, Paris, 2002); *Un Nirvana Cruel: poèmes 1980–2000* (Éditions Phi, Luxembourg, and Écrits des Forges, Quebec, 2000). Previous magazine & anthology publications include *@tached document,* CCCP (Cambridge, England), *Cimarron Review, Cream City, Earth's Daughters, 5 Trope, Gate* (Germany), *Golden Handcuffs Review, Intrait d'union: Bulletin de l'union des écrivains* (Paris), *Jacket* (Australia), *Journal of Literature & Aesthetics* (India), *Naropa University 25th Summer Writing Program Magazine, New York Arts, POG2, Samizdat, Sub Voicive Poetry* (London), *Sulfur, Taos Poetry Circus, Van Gogh's Ear* (Paris).

Manufactured in the United States of America
Book design by Sylvia Frezzolini Severance
New Directions Books are published on acid-free paper.
First published as New Directions Paperbook 955 in 2002
Published simultaneously in Canada by Penguin Books Canada Ltd.

Library of Congress Cataloging-in-Publication Data

Rothenberg, Jerome, 1931–
A book of witness : spells & gris-gris / Jerome Rothenberg.
p. cm.
ISBN 0–8112–1537–7 (acid-free paper)
I. Title.
PS3568.O86 B66 2003
811'.54—dc21

2002154638

New Directions Books are published for James Laughlin
by New Directions Publishing Corporation,
80 Eighth Avenue, New York, NY 10011

for Diane

This morning
all the voices in my dream
spoke with one voice.
I feel privileged to be here
among you.
From now on
we will live
on borrowed time.

Contents

Spells & Gris-Gris 51–100

Spells & Gris-Gris 1–50

Language belongs to the saint children.
They speak and I have the power to translate.

María Sabina

1
THE CASE FOR MEMORY

I was amok & fearless
twice deceived
for which I sought out
satisfactions
in a tree.   Too carelessly
I reached for love
& beaten down
I found you
in a froth or frenzy
spent my days around
the pan yards.
I would ask no help from those
whose trust is weak
but I would buy the latest
& the least.
I live for something practical
—the case for memory—
I set one foot into the space
the others leave abandoned.
Not your lord or slave
I meet you
in an equal clash of wills
& face you down.
I only touch the ground
on Sundays

2
THE BURNING HOUSE

It was always dark.
The red hole's
wetness threatened
the lost sheep.
Sharp exchanges
were not clearly heard.
Rivers did
not flow.
You did not defend
your brother.
We ascend
toward progress.
I scratch fire &
remove it from your throat.
I run out of
distant shadows
now that no one
tries to stop
the passage from a city
that is drowning.
You must dodge
the summer fire
to free your soul.
You cannot stand
back of the burning
house from which
strangers emerge
like wolves
to run you down.

3
WHERE GOD IS LIGHT

The lost in hell
among the rat-faced
killers.
I am with them.
Standing at the tunnel's mouth
the water underneath
I see the figures floating
raised in air
then pitched into the vortex.
Here where god is light
a brown globe
hangs above
a burning hell.
Eyes turn right.
Hieronymus (my namesake)
let me lift this picture
from your hands.
I cherish walking in your circles.
Do you think the light is wet?
Forget it little father
& go home.
Return the keys to management.
When someone asks
if you believe in god
turn cautious.
There are now angels everywhere.
Never look back.

I HAVE PAID THE PRICE & LOST

God of the universe
manqué
you issue from my mouth.
I watch you dying.
Muscles like flowers gather
at your throat.
You shake a wrist at me.
Your watchband comes apart
& freezes.
I can see you with a babe
propped on your lap
or else a lamb.
Old man with blisters
working against time
you plunge a knife
into my book.
The babe limp as a doll
tilts forward
gagging.
A man in chains
sucks
on a woman's breast.
Feet walk
without a body.
I have paid the price & lost.
And you?
Have you watched them play
the game of tribute?
And have you failed to pay
& won?

5
THERE IS A MAP INSIDE MY POCKET

I look for lights
under my fingers.
I will take them & will make
foolish minds wise.
Then when I flick my half closed eyes
your mouth will open wide
& I will sail by with my flags.
You will applaud me
when I scratch for cash
under your shadows.
I who am geared to tear down
what you build
your houses like your ashes
swept away.
I search the sky for you.
It rains.
The wind too warm for Sunday
sears my eyes.
There is a map inside my pocket
I can't read.
All day I tried to call you.
Where the bus stopped
people walked by
like the dead.
I knew your house was there
down by the corner.
A house without a bell
without a way to find your way
around it.

6
AN EMPTY BELL

I walk with you into
the little houses.
Rings slip through my hands.
You pierce your tongue
for love.
How bright the fields grow
yellow blue & red
this morning
where the owl's prey drops down.
Look at me.
Be first.
The others will come through
in shallow order.
Someone not a king
is fancier
a thief among a thousand
shattered crosses.
Elsewhere
broken columns
flutist on a hill
old man who lugs a basket
two old men who push
a stone door into place.
A line of walkers
riders
coming up the road.
I blow a whistle.
Then I bang your teapot
like an empty bell.

7
WHAT THE WORLD GIVES BACK

No one looks for garbage
underneath
your windows.
No one waits alone
& hears
the slow wave rising.
There are some who shadow us
for what we love.
Nightly the passengers
still blind me
while I bind their wounds.
I feel their final jabs
between the covers & the sea
no time for preening.
I watch my feet move
among the stars.
Everything we offer
to the world
is what the world gives back
without a thought
or breath.
Mythology as science
fact as trope.
I walk into a cavern
where a bear lies dead.
You can divine my words
because my words
ring true.
It doesn't matter
if the rhyme
is slant or straight.
I feel it on my tongue
my eyes
see through it.

8
A PREMONITION

It is a battle between
this & this.
An armageddon.
One pursues & hobbles
finds the ground rise up
to hurt him.
From the left a boat
so small
I would not think
a space was left
for sailing.
Later
we were on a mountain top
with strangers.
Tell me if my mind
was set
too firmly.
She who was our leader
slipped.
We had a premonition.
With his knife
the old man
cut his way
out of the room.
It ill behooves us
someone said
as though her words rang true.
A thousand bodies
hanging
from a thousand trees
ended the dream.

9
LIKE A WALL

Day by day
I watch the sidewalk.
Light builds up.
A man without a face
is still a man.
He is the victim
of his own
worst thoughts.
The light runs from his eye.
Robbed of its speed
it blinds him.
Every moment
is the last
before death ends it.
Launched through space
he stumbles
but he makes it back.
I can replace him
in my thoughts
like all the rest.
The secrets of arithmetic
are what he leaves me.
Open up the vents.
Your eye is dead.
Your mind is not your own.
Your fingers burn.
Your tongue speaks from your mouth
but no one listens.
It is too late to eat
or piss
however urgent.
Time spreads out between us
like a wall.
A radio in space
can't overcome it.

10
A REAL MAN

Mangled fingers
push the stones aside.
The scars run deep.
Hate suits
the human face
far better
than a mask.
The price of happiness
is wisdom.
Stones that interfere
with speech
will interfere with sleep
no longer.
Soon he wipes away
the stain.
The motor seems outrageous.
Back & forth
he walks.
I watch the fathers
growing
throwing caution to the winds.
My body hovers
in an air
the man can hold forever
in his sights.
I do not trust his way
of dealing.
He & I
are brothers
for this moment
only.
Watch his fingers closing.
He is a real man
when he murders
is he not?

11
EVERY NIGHT AT TEN

I slip through streets
hoping that a dog
won't bag me.
I turn my back to strangers
when my own skin
grows too hard.
I spend long nights
in mausoleums
like a prince.
When I bite the flesh
over my thumb
it bleeds.
I lost my fear of death
last summer
& I want to teach the trick
to all my friends.
Mine is a case of
double vision.
The taste arises
from my throat
& not
the other way around.
The way I cry
calls out for pity.
I struggle for a chance
to hide from sleep
but every night at ten
it runs me over.

THERE IS NEVER ENOUGH TIME

Above the clouds
is nothing
but a leprous
single star.   (B. Brecht)
The more I look at it
the less I feel.
I try to recollect. I shake
a distant hand
& pay for laughter.
The odds are heavily
against me.
There is never enough time.
When I place a foot
in the hot water
someone declares me lost.
I smile into a mirror
& my face
glares back.
A father holds his babe
up to the light.
Where will it lead us?
Heaven is no place for fools.
I run my fingers
through your hair
& feel the universe
shut down.

13
THE LAST FRIEND

The day the last friend
dies
we sit alone.
A visitor
from outer space
tries hard
to summon us.
Someone says
EAT DEATH.
I fish around for answers
but the questions
still won't come.
I take the small vial
from your pocket
sniff it & near die.
The police are negligent
at best.
Nor is there room for angels.
The storms drift in from Mexico
where once we roamed.
The way your chest
moves up & down
when breathing
is a clear response.
I want some reassurance:
that even when I die
the world goes on.

I AM MAD BY TURNS

When I close my eyes
I see them.
Never more & never clearer
than they were
before your heart broke.
I am mad by turns.
Those who lead me to the trough
can never
make me drink.
The time shines like a signal
from my wrist.
Every pattern you observe
will disappear
even those the stars make
in their long sleep.
Is that enough to please us?
I am moved to say it
moved too that Blackburn died so young
& Armand now.
I am waiting for everyone
to die.
For this the just man
spews but holds
his ground.
His strength too distant
to return   his hands
two pools of sweat.
He must resemble someone
I saw walking backwards
once   & up a flight of stairs
a tray of food
in gentle balance
letting go
& hurtling
to his death among
the thorns.

MORE THAN STARS

You did it
made me cry
in hemorrhage.
You were on my mind.
I ran to you
& bones broke.
I who was finger mad
now learned to live
ungloved.
Unglued I sucked the wind
into my glottis.
I could be split in two
not whole
the rage emptied my scrotum
& I sagged.
You signaled from the car
ahead of me.
The screen lit up
with buttons
that were more than stars.
An egg escaped.
It could have happened
all at once
but I
was ready.
I embraced a cat
& spattered.
How I do love to touch
that ancient keyboard
wet from sleep.
None of you asked my name
& I kept silent
balanced on a dime.
I would delude them all
by dialing backward.
The time is near
I told them.
Nobody living will escape.

A CRUEL NIRVANA

Half dead
is still alive
& half alive is too.
So keep it rolling
I declare.
The others mingle in a room
atop the city
where a fire burns.
They sing.
I sing among them.
Then I push my way through
with my thumbs.
I eke a living
from a stone.
Hard knocks are bound to follow.
I can hear
a water song
close by my ear
& track it
where it leads me.
It is summer
but the trees
are dead.
They vanish with
our fallen friends.
The eye in torment
brings them down
each mind a little world
a cruel nirvana.

ENHANCING THE PLEASURE

Every moment of rest
foreshadows your actions
the thrusts of your pelvis
in love
your urgings & mine.
Now your head swings loose
on your shoulders
disgorging.
The tips of your fingers
find weather
or hide in the cave
of your glove.
You pull back
when it hurts
enhancing the pleasure.
Conception follows
or death.
Then we run away
fearful of time
the mysterious movements
of planets
a gondola hanging in space
skin like ice.
Where desires tell tales
you welcome me into
your dreams.
I mark time to the sound
of your heart.
Then we swoon.

WHEN WE DO ONE PLUS TWO

There is no place for us
to live
except for your mind.
There is no house
a mile away
to which we can walk.
No room feels like my room
after the rain.
Strangers with sticks
follow our footsteps
every morning.
I crouch atop your mattress
like a dog
& feel its pressures.
I let your body tell me
if there is time.
When we do one plus two
the light sparks up
inside its box
& what we take from it
is an adjustment.
Here I force the water through
to flush their voices.
I make a hole down which
a foot slides
severed from its shoe.
I blow the air away
until the mirror
shows me your other face.
I call the gods to witness
& when they do
I let them die.

19
AT NIGHT

When the caravan
stops
I cut my way through
layers of
old rags.
The infants brush
against my
knotted forearm.
I feel the skeleton
inside my skin
& where
a heart lies beating.
They will come for me
at night
not strangers but
to beg me for my name
till I return it.

TO MAKE LIFE REAL

I have no name
but what
was left me.
Therefore voices
ring inside
my head
like little pearls.
I try to force them back
by talking dirty.
Someone stands there
as an enemy
to make life real.
I dream propellers
& a train that leaves
the station
never to return.
I am a friend to thieves.
With visitors
I skim through photographs
out of a lost past.
I hate the ones
who hate me
& will make them pay.
There is no end to music
when all is caught
on tape.
A birthday foremost
afterwards a grave.
Asleep & barely able
I stare them down
while in my thoughts I mark
their darker fate.

THE MESSAGES OF SLAVES

A finger reaches
to the bottom of my dish
& stalls there.
Fat accumulates
around the tip.
I like to kick off
any garments
that encumber me.
The pool in which I dip
turns red.
We suck each other's
breasts
like mothers.
These are the messages
of slaves
the little ones
your finger
plays with.
The ink runs down my page
unchanneled.
Every factory
more dirty
than the last.
I am caught between
too many circuits.
Life inside the hive
is like a dream
someone already dreamed
into existence.

BETTER THAN NUMBERS

Better than numbers
& more real
the heart beats bravely.
I long to hear it
even where
it hurts.
We give ourselves to counting
from first to last.
My foot pulls back.
You mark me with
a dog's snout
eyes dark with kohl
& hair with henna.
I ask no more from you
than what I earn.
Still I try hard to cry
& burn my hair.
I stay aloof to strangers
the ones who kill me
with their eyes
the others whom I ask
to lick my fingers.
The rest is what an army
left behind.
Running through gardens.
I watch my body fall
into a tunnel.
It is my body still
alight &
shining
like a giant egg.
With fingers
I can count the time
but once without them
I am doubly lost.

IN THE STARS

I'd like to keep my hat & coat
reasonably clean
on the walk from New York
to California.   (L. Niedecker)
But what intrudes on me
are gritty pebbles
& a line of teeth.
A man like you
I wear
my spectacles
with a regard for dirt.
I find it everywhere
the more I look
but Saturdays I turn from it
fearful to learn.
It's in the stars
they tell me
or in the wind.
A small car stalls
in public
humming.
The señoras
struggle
with the señoritas
earth with worms.
I murmur:
lead & I will follow
down a country road.
I am a nomad
& I name a book
for doing only
what I had feared to.

DESPAIR IS NEVER UNIVERSAL

I will force smiles
from tyrants. I will wake silences
with screams. My breathing
clouds my eyes. I jump
until my mind forgets
the nightmare that was mine
from birth. I rub the spot
love springs from
eager for the lips to part.
I beg no more from them
than I can give.
I host a banquet
of rank fruit. What soothes me
smoothes my mind.
I ask for no one to be
close the while I
search the ground for pilfer.
I would declare
my innocence but fear it
in my heart. Despair
is never universal
until it is.

25
THE KINGS OF WATER

The world below the waves
is where I live. I come there
nightly. Someone bundles me
until the breath
runs safely through my lungs.
The limbs that move beneath me
are my own. The arms
are mine. My body is a bullet
not a sieve.
I beg the friends
be still . . . be penitent.
However dark it gets
I see by touching.
Those who drown are not
the kings of water
but its slaves.
I form a taste for islands.
Up is down for me.
A corridor of lights, a floor
of flutterings
I keep them to myself
imperious.
I see you looming up
& dream your name. It fits you
like a caul.*
The world we leave
is full of messages.
When the time arrives for rapture
do not be left behind.

* a cowl

I WILL NOT SAVE THE WORLD

I like to cross
these borders. They take place
between the dead & dead.
I make my mind up
to be honest
only I fail to meet
their expectations.
I will not save the world.
The power in my blood
runs through my shoe.
I have never known fatigue
but know it now. I whistle
& the dog sits still
& ponders.
Nobody else is resting
or in love.
The taste of death is in my mouth.
I suck it like an arm
until it breaks me.
It is the fate of animals
& birds
the small lives left behind.
The children in the woods
run by like children.
I hide under a blanket
sick with counting.
Two & two are five
but two times two
is always four.
Call me tomorrow
—says the voice—
& I will call you back.
*I am a net for all
voracious fish*
& long for hell.

(E. Södergran)

I PRACTICE DYING

I tell myself again
I have a headache.   (L. Aragon)
Even while sitting still
I mine it
& it opens wide for me.
Above my head planes fly
with double wings.
My hand clutches a pencil.
I am wet. I plan to break out
from my flooded cell.
I watch the ghost of Louis Aragon
walking in the courtyard
spitting
searching for abominable meaning.
My hands are on her belly
as in life. My eyes
skip over what I cannot see.
I practice dying
as the time draws nigh.
Stones press into my feet
the more I walk
then when the morning starts
the streets are dark
with strangers.
I am riding on a ferris wheel
& see it all.
It little comforts me
to hear their songs
& less to sing them.
I tell myself
I have to get some air.
The songs are songs
the words are useless
but persist.
I cannot drive them
from my mind.
A thousand drowned
that was never born.

IN DEFIANCE OF THE DEAD

A thousand drownded
that was never born.   (J. Ritchie)
Their faces stun me
with their eyes.
Alive & anxious
I run to stations
to make sure the trains
arrive on time.
I am aware that what
the body does for *love*
is sometimes *not.*
I celebrate
reversals.
I watch a funeral
somewhere at sea.
I am more calm than when
the buddhist bells
ring from the house tops
in defiance of the dead.
I could have sparkled then
but wouldn't.
Someone counts them off
by thousands
in a backwards dream.
All who drowned before
stay drowned.
The universe flows past
its boundaries
with no end in sight.
I see the sun plunge
like a comet
see you at the glass door
crouching.
Where it strikes the sea
a pale tsunami
breaks against the shore.

A MEDICINE THAT KILLS ME

I am the victim of
my mind. It hurts
the more I probe it.
Like the rest of you I have
a sickness
no one can see.
I take a medicine
that kills me.
Someone puts a finger
to my mouth.
I can no longer wait
for everyone to die
inside me. In the end
there is no end
to speak of.
The people I most love
surround me
waving flags.
I am borne aloft by them
a fearless king.
I can only pay for it
with desperation
& a smile
no one can understand.
Tonight the future
opens brightly.
The aim of medicine
is neither health
nor profit
but the right to die.

TO SLOW THE PASSAGE

Like cyber monkeys
into mindless space
the friends rush past me.
I kick the dirt aside
& go in hiding.
Over my head I sometimes
wear a torso
sometimes a fleur-de-lys.
I am not supple.
Rather I seek a place
meant to be small
but open to the wind.
Trippers & askers surround me.
I jubilate.
I gabble.
I implore.
The earth is friable
& falls
short of my vision.
I walk between
two friends
to slow the passage.
I write for science
with my thumbs.
The aim of health is medicine.
The monkey's scream
is not the monkey
but the end's the same for all.

31
THIS DOES ME PROUD

I drop a book
face up
& settle into
righteous thought.
I am the most relaxed
of all
in my identity.
My name is set
before you. See the lights
that flicker from
the silver tray.
And see her polished fingers.
One is red, the others
jet black.
I walk safely
when I turn another
corner.
It is not my choice
to meet you
but I can
& know it.
Sometimes someone
brings me underground
& lets me stay
close to the circuits.
Otherwise
I find myself besieged
by helicopters
in a line above
the temple.
I am so pleased to meet you.
Shake my hand
& smile.
This does me proud.

September 1999
Vienna

THE CURSE WAS STRONGER

I was relieved
that there were streets
& people.
Every time the train stopped
I re-set my watch.
I ran for
office but the time
ran faster.
Later when it rained
I wrapped a sheet around
the engine.
I offered friends
my presence
& they took it
like a life
they looked at
from without.
I wished them
all the best
but in the end
the curse was stronger.
I dismiss their
humble gestures
at whatever cost.
I need a place
to stand
so I can move the world.
I laugh a lot
because it hurts me
when I turn
to leave.

THE SEARCH FOR TRUTH

About myself I
need know nothing.   (S. Beckett)
I am more than satisfied
to sit here
waiting for the phone to ring
or to stay quiet.
At night I dream of friends
no longer living.
A side of beef
floats in the air
over our table.
The search for truth
is all I have
yet I discard it.
With my fingers
I can make bells
ring. The role of sex
is crucial until
hunger
drives it out.
We are on a football field
with grass
the color of old hair.
I am an absent particle.
Someone with a stomach
filled with worms
watches us breathe.
The name they write down
on the blackboard
isn't mine.
I climb out of my empty hole
& fight for air.
My legs are carrying
another's body.
Life is opening
at a distance
something we still can't see.

WHEN SLEEP DRAWS NIGH

The hope of life is all
that makes life live.
Often I pine for it
though it grows cold.
My thoughts visit a home
where no one dwells.
The old dilemma grows.
I feel the ground crumbling
under my heels.
Nothing returns to me
once it has gone.
I shrug my shoulders
like a fool.
I spit into a cloth
spread on the earth.
I make a little
sexual sound
when sleep draws nigh.
No one is calmer here
than in a court
with columns, beggars
awash in dreams,
a dark sun overhead.
The city where we came to rest
was Paris
half a century ago.
I see a window opening
a crack & spilling feathers
in the street.
A mouth fills up
with seed
until it bursts.
Only when blind
I take a chance
although it pains me.
I dream of sharing time
with them but know
it won't return.

I BELIEVE IN THE MAGIC OF GOD

I believe in the magic of god   (J. de Lima)
& in fire. Somebody
dangles a key on the steps.
From a hole in my chest
eyes stare out.
I run into a circle
of friends
little men with pale lips
& soft fingers.
I signal new forms of expression.
The way sand shapes hills
& water shapes fountains.
I am in their hands completely
helpless as a babe
unless the babe command the world
sending a stream of
feathers
back to earth.
A prince he is & dances
between rivers
then rides a shining rocket
to the upper air.
It brings the wolves to me
to eat out of my hand.
The streets of Rome
signal a fresh
disaster. I am one
a pope would deign to speak to
when I wave my arms.

I FEEL A SURGE OF POWER

I am the mother of my father
moaning   in a crone's voice
she is seated to my right
a shawl with stones & bones
falls to the floor.
I feel a surge of power
like a prophet.
I can tell the time
not by a watch
or compass
but by a hand shake.
I walk by crawling
on my elbows
so that my feet can sleep.
The distance from the ground
is logged
in fathoms   space
is not a word I fear
but time is.
I am both near & far away
both man & dog.
I open up my hand & show you
what remains.
The vapor in the air.
The moisture.
Someone wraps a cloth
over my eyes.
It's two o'clock.   (V. Mayakovsky)
And now it's three.
The synagogue is sealed
she says.
I feel the darkness breathing
like a perfect friend.
I am the bride & bridegroom.
I am the first & last.

37
GOING CRAZY

I was
relaxed from
going crazy.
I ignored
a happiness
unknown.
Before it all
came down I
dug myself a hole
emptied of
water.
I dissolved
the boundaries
that held me close
like sex.
I put down
anyone
who tries to
put me down.
I ruminate
a proper way
to let time pass.
I take from others
what they need
& watch their deaths
leap naked
from their eyes.
I sit where space
is tightest.
I fret over
the mysteries
of being born.

I WEAVE A CIRCLE THRICE

Electricity runs
from my beard.
I shift from there
into a yellow place
convulsed but not
convulsive.
I learn to dance
with dibbiks.
In a straight line
the passengers salute me
with their eyes.
I lick a little metal plate
a ring of sugared ice
over my lips. I trudge
with hands at sides
resigned to numbness.
The dead hare in the dream
escapes its forest
it is too late to call a neighbor
to stalk it until it drops.
This is the message that I forged
in my capacity as charmer.
I go in & out of doors.
I open windows
gently
when it's time to leave.
I weave a circle thrice
for poets after us
to enter.
I will turn my angry words
into an imprecation
a spell I'll cast
& that you'll follow.

THE FIRE DEEP INSIDE

My penis in the shape
of my own heart
rests on the pillows.   (F. Picabia)
I taste a liquor never brewed
out of your lips.
The generals are gathering.
They stare into each other's eyes
through mirrors.
With a display of wounds
we signal them
& turn away. I am the last
because the fire
deep inside
burns till it's morning.
Poetry is made in bed
for some   for me
the call of life is stronger.
I walk & see my shadow
hanging upside down
with yours. The way
your mouth says *I*
is just like mine.
I multiply
the little portion
that your fingers
spill.
I cannot comprehend
the way men kill
or laugh. I will not
vouch for them.
There is a space to burrow in
under the covers.
The way he wants to kiss
while vomiting
is part of life. The way
he calls on death
trumpets his own.

I TAKE A PAGE OUT OF YOUR BOOK

I neither run
nor dance
but stand upright.
Someone comes by
to wipe my face
with creams.
The buzzard is a bird
we only see
in architecture
hidden by iron sticks
& faceless.
I know a passageway
leads to the Seine
but still can't find it.
Instead of time
I have the sense
of falling backwards.
The little man
inside the frame
is me   the one outside
grows old.
The party on the way
to Normandy
stops on the quay side.
I adjust my wristwatch
but the hands
keep falling off.
I take a page out of your book.
The pockets of my coat
fill up with water.
To have you watch your step
assures my own
though barely.
I want to tell the throngs
to stop but know
they won't.

I PREFER A POEM WITH SPACES

I like to crack my words
between my teeth.
I tie my hair back
in a knot
& little care
how well it suits me.
The unearthing of a coin
under the streets
leaves us all shrieking.
I can pretend to think all thoughts
at once.
Seldom for me
is frequent
for my friends.
I prefer a poem with spaces
to a block of prose.
I do not mention roses.   (G. Stein)
The thrill of climbing
makes me wring my hands
in glee.
You see me
& you
look away.
You ask me to be cautious.
I can reply to you
if time allows
if not I can stand still.
A poor girl reaches out her hand
but I have nothing left
for her   not rhyme
nor reason.
We are all feckless
when it comes to love
still more to justice.

In the dream the child speaks Russian
& is otherwise
a cat. I have such trust
in her I let her
guide me.
That is who I am
& what I crave.
I practice magic with my lips.
A book of mine is buried
in an egg
but still I read it.
I am the tamer of wild beasts
& you their mistress.
A pitiful procession
fills the streets
the men on shoulders of the men
but static   stuck
like wasps in syrup.
I learn a smiling language
where the words are pink.
I soar to status of a father
not in love   & not
the prince of love.
Many times I gamble
then I throw the cards aside
& beg for air.
It is eight a.m. in Paris
but still dark.
When the sun ignites
the broken window
will you again be here for me
or must we part?

I COUNT IT BY A THOUSAND

A thousand times a thousand
is too much to count.
Knowing that that is so
I count it by a thousand
but soon fall back.
Sometimes I lose my numbers.
I who was tall at birth
am shrunken
like your thumb.
The counting stops at four
on one hand
but the other brings it
up to ten.
The strangers mark my arm
& find it wanting.
I am a head that speaks
a belly always full
between my legs a humming
shakes the air.
I do not count with it
or by it.
You hand me papers
& a watch. You count the sound
a bell makes
when it's nearly dawn.
I am the man with fingers.
Count the days with me
& tremble.
It is not enough to say
a thousand   still not enough
to play the clown or be
the father of the world.
You can count on me
for love.   I take it
but forget
what words to speak.

IT IS A DAY OF MIRACLES FOR ME

I am the man who gives relief.
I am the big man.   (R. Estrada)
It is a day of miracles
for me   for you
a day of frozen motion.
I am alive with atmosphere.
My hands are red.
My eyes are red & white.
I walk into a pit with buildings
rooftops like a crown
a ring of air around them.
I burn hot & cold.
I am the tall & handsome one.
The man who gets up early.
I am the dawn.
The trembling reaches from my arm
into the place
where dogs & men assemble
& where a siren howls
to mark the noonday.
I assign a path from there
to here. The mystery
is all contained in
speaking. Then the little silences
surround my words
like poetry. I breathe them
in & out until
they turn to points of light
blinding my eyes.
In darkness I will make
my sound felt.
I will make your bones
resound.

I GIVE UP MY IDENTITY

My name is smaller
than it sounds.
I work & polish it
until a light
shines through.
I thrust a thorn under
my tongue.
I drop the little stones
behind me. Striding
I can feel my height extend
up to the rafters.
My voice is thin,
still thinner
is the space between
my footsteps
& the earth.
I do not want you
calling me
except at the allotted
times. I scratch my head
because I know
it's empty. Hot & cold
are equal terms.
I give up my identity
to write to you.
The notice on the board says:
Stay at home
Be vigilant
The aim of medicine is
medicine.
I can hardly wait until
tomorrow.
Signals everywhere
are fraught
with terror.
In the deepest
waters spread around
the globe

there is a sense
of life so full
no space exists
outside it.
I will go on writing
till I drop
& you can read my words
beyond my caring.

I IS THE FIRST WORD

I is the first word
spoken, slim
& long
the perfect particle.
It is absent from my speech
if I avoid it
but it invades my mind.
I call myself by other names
none of them active.
I stands along with *me*
as who I am.
I pull myself apart
sooner or later
& where *I* comes to rest
is where I dwell.
Be faithful to your sense of me.
I is an other   gaunt
& somewhat turned
into the light.
I threatens to return,
is hungry now
for power
as for love.
He is my own, becomes
my shadow
dog.
I reach a hand to him
& freeze.
I cannot speak
without him
though we try.

I DARE NOT STARVE

I am at the top of
my disgorge. I aim
for stars
but miss my mark at last
& flail.
I am the man who springs
a nectarine
to smooth you.
I dare not starve.   (Wen Yiduo)
Thereby I sleep on cardboard.
Forced to scramble
I am naked
down my back.
I snake my turn.
Giving it slack takes time
I do not crave
or offer.
The less that's left for living
the more I stake.
I have a pack of cards
to trade
for others while
I coil.
Never too sure I scan
my fractals on
the stranger's screen.
I supervise palazzos.
I am always flying but
prefer to ride
by rail. Observe me
where I flaunt
credentials.
Once so buoyant
I would crow
& split my sides
by inches.
I am lame but limber
the hungry dog

who wets your circle.
I enter it with lamps
& seeds.
I bend my frame & say:
*I did not mean
to entertain you.*

.

THE END IS THE BEGINNING

The cylinder grinds against
another cylinder.
It fills my head with wheels
& makes a gnarly sound
like sailing through
the ether. I am halfway
sick & sunken
hoping to right myself
before it's over.
This is the song I weave
because a text
is like a garment.
I would have my body
dressed in words
after I die. I write it out
with wires
that I read from right
to left. Pallaksch
is perfect German
more & more. Tomorrow
someone rides a bike
under the stars.
A boulevard is better.
Metal cries out loud
the more we sound it.
Smart is dumb.   (K. Schwitters)
What's seen is understood.
I tuck the little balls away
& screen them.
I will meet you on the train.
Good morning.
The end is the beginning
of the end.

A TOWN CALLED METER

There is a town called meter
north of Spain.
In it the dead still live
& I have seen them,
who am hungrier than them
not angrier.
I stand among them
with my forged
credentials, calling
on the rest to follow
suit. A bunch of drifters
rubs against me
men with iron spoons
gouging my heart.
I stumble after them
into a town square
sunk below sea level
hard & dry.
A gay parade
files past me
inching up the steps.
I stop a while
my feet in broken flight
over the stones.
The night flows from my eye
the day holds back.
I learn to mimic birds
caught in the brambles.
I have a stark
vocabulary
letting my heart keep time,
my throat in rapture
crying out to you:
the mask! the mask!
in perfect rhythm.

I can't say who I am   (A. Baraka)
but go for it
& speak
as if I knew it.
Time is half the story
so is death.
I run from shadows
to avoid old people
maddened by God.
I follow animals
whose eyes at night
mirror my face.
Seeing myself asleep
I touch my arm.
I celebrate
new forms of sex.
I am frantic
knowing that nobody
has a way out
or a face
more marked than
mine.
I was not
born live.   (J. Holzer)
The case for memory
grows weaker
day by day.
The more I know myself
the less I am.
I hold on to a name
because it suits me
but the voice behind it
never was my own.

Spells & Gris-Gris 51-100

Do I contradict myself?
Very well then I contradict myself,
(I am large, I contain multitudes.)

Walt Whitman

I COME INTO THE NEW WORLD

Voices are dumb until
I speak for them.
Knowing the sound
I find myself between
two fires. One
is dark green, one
the color of my mind
asleep. I come into
the new world
where the thought of death
no longer rankles.
It will be good to be
a stranger always
to know the terms by which
we visit   back & forth
& sideways.
In the morning I will wear
a suit with shoulders
big as boards. My clothes are
silver plastic.
When I step into the car
it starts to fly.
I play games with
children
where I make
a nose
into an ear.
Like a clock my heart
moves closer
to the burning babe
& stays there.
I will now count
the century
by ones & twos.
This morning
all the voices in my dream
spoke with one voice.
I feel privileged to be here

among you.
From now on
we will live
on borrowed time.

January 1, 2000

IT IS A SHAME TO WATCH MY FACE

I am unmarked
but fearful
always in search of hope.
Instead of sleep
I wander
turning the miles
between us
into days.
I am a stranger on
the garden path
the glass walls looming large
to every side.
It is a shame to watch
my face   to see it
running through your hands
like jelly.
I am my own
dark friend
a shadow set against
a darker shadow.
I hear a sound
like pianos
buried in the earth.
The pressure of my feet
against the pedals
opens a flood.
A carrousel is bobbing
up & down.
The happy singer
enters paradise
with seven others.
I regret not being there
to bury him
less for his sake than for
the etiquette.
The tygers of wrath
are wiser than
the horses
of instruction.   (W. Blake)

KILL OR BE KILLED
is scrawled across
your window.

53
I HOLD DARK MATTER

I hold dark matter
in my thoughts
like ancient prophecy.
On Mondays
I adjust the hanging
clock. The galaxies
are deeper images
than once we knew.
Their absent light
confounds me.
Now the unreal
dwarfs the real.
A woman
like the sun
cries out
in shallow French.
I feel my arms
grow lame
& work
against me.
The moon
glows red
Great distances
are mine. I plot
their numbers
but I know
that every universe
contains another.
There is no end in sight
& no beginning.
The stars stay dark
in mirrors
until your fingers
counting them
have dropped away.

WHAT WAS BEGUN IN ANGER

I succumb to
all the visions.   (N. Brossard)
Happily
my mind possesses
what I lost.
My days
are in a final
order
known to me alone.
I wind the bed sheets
over a fat knee.
I eat & then I swim.
I turn more corners
than a walk
from home
would have allowed.
I set loose stones
in motion
one atop
the next.
I wonder
why one thief
hangs
backwards.
The mist of morning
makes the scene
look blue.
From sleep I beckon.
While you stand in place
I race ahead.
I call on history
the way some call
on God.
What was begun
in anger
now brings peace.

55
AS FROM A DISTANT HEIGHT

From my fingers
none escape.
I lock forgiveness
in a tree.
As from a distant height
I drop a barrel down
& watch it
splinter.
My hand evades its glove
the matchbox quality
that lends it heat.
I plot a path for sheriffs
wry defenders
of the law of balances.
So am I plugged
but signal back
& plug the others.
Again I see myself
in danger.
I am twice in place.
The food uneaten
in the dish
slides down my throat.
Seldom do I dare
to count with these
my rock-ribbed deputies
but time does fly
like grit.
I knock a drink back
in a western bar
& sail to China.
I have no wish to continue
my debate with men. (E. Dorn)

A GIANT FOR THE MOMENT

Man wolf to man
I cried out
in a childhood rant.
The temperature of bodies
raised a qualm
I couldn't conquer.
Mice inched by in squadrons
step by step.
I was your angel
guide & buddy
up a street
with mottled ferns.
I felt so sad.
P.S. So lonely blooming.   (J. Joyce)
Time didn't return
but crumbled. Motors ran
at night
& split the clouds.
The prey sprang back.
I raised an arm
scraping the sky
a giant for the moment.
Closer to home
I faltered.
I was amok no more.
A crazy gambler
with no regard for pain
I drew the angry ones
around me.
I was a friend to wolves
at last   the dark one
longer than this couch
who touched me
with his tongue
the while my heart stood still.

I-SONGS EXIST

i-songs exist,   (I. Christensen)
& I have sought them,
playing an empty hand.
i is your mother,
is a good day
& also not.
i equals nothing
in the game of numbers
where it is also ten
& jew.
i is a womb
a belly
something stolen
heart & hand.
i eats
& will be eaten.
i is a habitation.
i is go & good.
i is a power.
i is to God
a question.
i is willing.
i is i-am
but stands confused.
i is a name for ice.
i is an end.

A LUCKY DAY

I pull my shirt up
hoping to exploit
the skin. A lucky day
is beckoning
the clock stands still.
I pull the plug
a dozen times
& count the whispers.
I am happiest
the more I sleep.
If all pans out
the keys will end up
safe in hand.
I will walk with you
into a garden
festooned
with the color
blue.
I am a wunderkind again
& you
are she who sits
beside me.
Tall men beat the bushes
beat their chests
but do not beat the rap
that time inflicts.
I am a hired courier
& bring a message
for the dead.
Tonight the banks close early
while your cash runs out.
I will arrive in time
in spite of traffic
& will pretend to pay.

I AM NOT A NATIVE OF THIS PLACE

I am not a native of this place   (Yoshimasu G.)
nor yet a stranger.
With the rest of you
I hunt for shade
my boots half off
to let the air through.
My head is on my shoulders
& is real.
I plant cucumbers
twice a year
& count the bounty.
Often I read
the papers
standing.
I am clean & pure.
I carry buckets
from the pond
more than my arms can bear.
Under a full moon
fish appear
like flies in amber.
The words of foreigners
invade my thoughts.
The hungry hordes
surround me
wailing through their beards.
My fingers tingle
feigning speech.
I have a feeling
that my tongue
speaks words
because my throat
keeps burning.

I MAKE MY WAY BY STEALTH

I hemorrhage & threaten
sleep. You wake averted
pale-faced
chasing phantoms
down the sky.
We look at every mirror
as a mere memento.
Mirages have arisen
& we swim in them.
I make my way by stealth.
In a house of children
no one reigns
or sleeps. The walls
start at the floor
& touch the ceiling.
I walk into a palace
like a hangar
where a candle is the only
light. A distant voice
assumes a shape
& many colors.
Happy is the pilot
in his cage
the glory of his parachute
in splendid motion.
He stares at us with love.
What hope is there
for us to soar
beyond him?
We delight in answering
your question
with a question.
The master of this house
plays happy music.
Bang it on the player piano
as in days gone by.

EAGER TO BREAK THROUGH LANGUAGE

I proceed along a path
that others
make for me
before they die.
The winds blow in from space.
I still do not exist   (N. Mandelstam)
but with a name like theirs
I play the game of *being*.
Eager to break through language
& touch life
I crack my head against
a mirror.
I hack at a false body
with a stick
pushing the flames apart
until the heart appears.
It is imperative to plant a garden
to share a common fate
with those called creatures.
Proud possessors
of a *geist*
they turn from me
the more I beckon.
I can no longer
face the music
though no one asks me
if I can.
I meet you backwards
out of shame.
The Baltic beckons.
Knowing
that the dead possess
a terrace
I ask permission to attend
the bride.
They call for silence
while my ear fills up
with grace.

62
I LIVE IN DUNGEONS

I live in dungeons
like a serf
my hand clutched
in my hand
to quell the shaking.
I am a scavenger
a brother
to my naked lord.
Anointed
I am eager to reverse
positions.
I no longer judge you
by your deeds
but when the clocks run down
I rush to meet you.
Blood & steel
are mine.
I need them
& they share
a function
with my own
Beware.
Beware.
The blade moves slowly
down my line of sight
& blinds me.
I am a little soldier
in my termite world
ready to kill

Schloss Kromborg
Helsingore
19.iv.00

63
I WILL NOT EAT MY POEM

I kill for pleasure
not for gain.
A man much more
than you   my hands
find knives
& flash them.
I am guilty
in my works
while in their eyes
I seek redemption.
I find myself
forgotten
angry at the thought
of bread. *I will not
eat my poem*   (A. Artaud)
*much less be raped
by it.* I have a home
but sit with others
shirtless, waiting
for the moon to rise.
I am a warrior
grown old.
The number on my ticket
tells the time.
I seldom wash
& wear a string
around my throat
until it crumbles.
Save yourself for love
the fool advises
& the wise man murmurs
Spill it now!
*Your glass is never
empty!*
I see your arm
the color of
wild lilacs.

It is not too late
for memory.
Days together are
like days apart.

64

A CALENDAR THAT FLUTTERED

I lived apart
from what was
forming.
I bartered
photos of
the dead.
Soon everything
caved in & I
emptied my throat
till I
felt cleaner.
I tore a
calendar that
fluttered like
girls' sex.
I will condemn
the world
because it talks of
love but doesn't.
I pack the
little bag I have
& start a journey.
I stop the world
just long enough
so that they think
they will not die
inside their rooms.
I crave a
mansion for
my throne.
I tremble at
the opportunity
of omni-
presence.

65
I ARRIVE IN PARIS

I meet with
old companions.
Lately
they & I are always
waiting
to be heard.
I engage with you
in angry sports
& marvel
how a single image
fills the square.
Crowds roar
& frighten
those whose memories
are cruel.
I arrive in Paris
& enter a train station
like the Gare de l'Est.   (A. Breton)
Thieves pause at windows
to address me.
We face each other
through the bars.
I carry papers from
another town
proving the need
to witness.
A bearded head
cut from its body
placed in the window of
a butcher's shop
the blood still red.
I want to speak
to it the way
a child speaks
but my eyes & lips
stay shut
from too much breathing.

THE VOICE INSIDE

I fart because
the voice inside
is outraged.
I discharge my oracles.
*I am not oblivious
to free words.*   (R. Owens)
The man who ushers me
barks like a monkey
in the half light.
I despair to look down
at a precipice
or at a sucking partner.
Tickles attract
like giggles.
I attach a faucet
to my mouth
so I can spew
unhindered.
I split a piece of wood
& at its core
I spot a stranger's
visage.
I shake with anger
when your face
touches my own.
I draw a naked body
on the street.
My fingers crack.
I hear a heart beat
wildly
that I guess is mine.

THEREFORE I AM

In a time of peace
I look for turmoil
never at rest.
I can imagine worlds
outside of worlds
& in between.
Each time I strike
the keys
a new world issues
from my fingers.
I am what I sweat.
I think & faint
from thinking.
Therefore I am
not only now
but every time increasing
when I think.
My brain is mayonnaise
& carries me
to distant futures.
I should be an eager christian
hungry for salvation   (S. Ortiz)
but my dreams don't scan.
I part the dirt.
I see the glass in front of me
darken with words.
I aim a question at
the universe
but a trillion others answer
in its place.

68
I AM WHERE YOU DROPPED ME

I baptize you
for centuries of
centuries

(M. Wittig)

& watch you flail.
You wrestle me
to death.
I see a pair of you
as high as
any house.
In less time
than it takes
to stumble
I am where you dropped me.
May I touch
your thin walls
with my pleas?
I am a wounded cur
a hound dog
famed in song
& deed.
You caravan the future
on my back.
I welcome you
knowing the odds
but play them.
Short or tall
I am the one who walks
beside you.
I have a rage for size
& take your measure.
Your hand is knocking
at my door.
I hear you, knowing
if I turn the key
the world will break
in sevens.

69
IN NERVAL'S TOWER

I play the prince
in Nerval's tower.
On a crooked swing
I like to soar
then click my heels.
I owe a paragraph
to those I love
fathers who taught us
how to fail.
A dish is doubly good
when salted.
I run sideways
praying for the ground
to settle down.
Dancers accost me
halfway home.
At the edge of Nevsky Prospekt
bandaged   fearful
Mishkin extends an arm
& pulls me down
ecstatic
to his face.
I spar with visitors
less keen than me.
I turn a buckle
outwards. Am I right
to dance for him
& does it heal?
No answer from the floor.
I take my time
& in the middle of my trance
he enters
with his hair
aflame.

70
BECAUSE I'M FOREIGN

I see you
better than you do
because
I'm foreign.   (A. Notley)
In what was once
my town I grope
& grovel   bloody
ribbons flaring
from my arms
my hair
aflame.
I lope behind
my dog
while keening.
Klansmen hassle me
with staves.
My mouth repeats
their dread words
calmly
shreds them on my tongue.
I have no qualms
but live with satisfaction
deep in sleep.
Beware of fallen lines
the sign says:
Death along the tracks
among the lost.
I aim a spell at someone
for a price. The word *botanica*
is crystal clear.
It bothers me to be here
babbling   lonesome
every time it rains.
More sure than gris-gris
in a foreign clime
my end draws nigh.

CURSING THE LIGHT

I walk the stupid
last mile
into heaven
cursing the light
that blinds me.
I reach up
& drive an owl
from its perch.
My clothes cling to my flesh.
I lift my fire
where my hand should be.   (C. Coolidge)
My watch
explodes
as if the gift
of time
were now annulled
I open up
my mouth & hear
a multitude
of voices.
I grow afraid of singing.
In the water
sound seeps through
my skull.
I lace my shoes
& tie them
to a hitching post
adrift in space.
My ghosts cry into tubes
like cell phones
pressed against my ears.
The view from paradise
appalls me. I turn
my back & ponder
fearful to be understood.

I LOSE THE SOUND THAT MUSIC MAKES FOR ME

I seek a
dark trace
that is running from
my eye.
I would have died
without it.
Phantoms spilled it out
& said I had
no use
for it.
It gives me pleasure
too the more
I think of it
& run the risk of
living life
without it.
If my mouth
shuts down I
lose the sound
that music
makes for me.
I cry aloud
my final crack
at wisdom.
But the voice
inside me
has another
voice behind it
I can hear
when dreaming.
Something tastes
for me.
My mouth makes
funky music
while my fingers
fail.

I SPEAK IN TONGUES

A child's hand
reaches out
for bread
or money.
I pull the hair out
from my ears.
Sundays
I walk with gangs
of children.
I am more an urchin
than a little man
or woman
with a beard.
I speak in tongues
so no one
understands. Friends die
in distant cities.
I keep walking through
the world   enough
to reach the moon &
circle backwards.
I become a star of
radio & films.
My dimpled features
fit as well
onto the tiny screen.
The tongues of men & angels
are my own. I speak
for multitudes
of dolphins *bing bong*
goes the bell. My heart
stands still.

74
THE MIRACLE OF DEATH

I kiss every
phallus   (Takahashi M.)
hoping to find
God.
I draw a needle
through my flesh
& holler.
When the clocks run down
I meet my true love.
Someone sits here
in the dark
& cuts her toenails.
The bride of Hitler—
is she not
a happy dear?
I let her ride me
like a dog.
I want no men around me
& no women
either.
I declare myself
the master spirit
eager to be splayed.
I run & prattle.
I will not be moved.
How much it pains me
to be last or least.
I tear dark letters
from a page &
wear them
on my skin.
The miracle of death
is only
that it sets us free.

HISTORY IS WHAT I LIKE TO CALL IT

Where will I take
my final bow?
I wait for hungry mouths
to beckon   try to
force dead nature
down their throats.
I make big towns
grow out of
small ones. History
is what I like
to call it.
I am also high on
mathematics.
Days divide & I
lose patience.
Time is money.
Never dive into
a pool
that's empty.
I can ride a rig
into the heart of
nowhere   dream of
muchachitas
till I die.
Like me the man
with arms tied
hides behind
a column.
Blood has made
his hands
& feet
turn black.
My eyes swell with
the pain
of being human.
Nothing changes
even if the train arrives
on time.

76
A MISSAL LIKE A BONE

Link by link
I can disown
no link.   (R. Duncan)
I search the passage
someone sends
& find a missal
like a bone.
My hands are white with sweat.
I lay my burden down
the ground below me
shrinking.
The more my fingers ply
these keys   the more
words daunt me.
I am what a haunt
averts, what you who once
spoke from my dream
no longer tell.
The book is paradise.
An odor is a clue
to what was lost.
I seek & speak
son of a father
with no home or heart.
I bantered with a friend
that there are speeds
beyond the speed
of light.
I spun around.
The calculus of two
plus two,
the mystery of
false attachments,
still persists.
I settled for
a lesser light   a circumstance
found that my words
rang true.

I LEAVE NO TIME FOR PLEASURE

I am often on a perch
from which I spy
the headlands.
I dig out furrows
with my nails.
I chop the legs off birds.
My work is keen
& feeds me.
I take a squad out to the woods
& beat them. Surly
like a swede
I leave no time for pleasure.
I parade for God.
I pull a tree out by the roots
uncovering a mountain.
I roll a truck
over a trail of tears
then land it in
a chuckhole.
You are near to me
& hear
the blood course through
my veins.
I raise a post & force it
deep into the soil.
There is a smell like tar
that swells my throat
a cavalcade of men at work
& grunting.
I throw a quarter in the air
hoping it won't
return to earth.
Six o'clock is never easy.
I am what I am
& you are watching me
with scorn.

I AM THANKFUL FOR YOUR WORDS

I smear my thighs
with honey.
I am thankful for your words
though never certain
what they mean.
I count on steamy days
to give me pleasure.
I sit with radios
& twist the dials until
a sigh comes forth.
I am your vulva, feather, feather   (A. Schwerner)
& I turn to you for grace.
Dreams are mine
& kindle
while I stoke the coals.
I prepare myself
by fasting.
Mornings I settle
for a voucher.
I seek out a body
not like mine
yet rife with holes
& odors.
A mold forms on my glasses.
I stretch out an arm
& touch a railing.
I let my flesh succumb
to oils   sweet myrrh
is on my shelf
the warmth of caravans
& distant climes.
I am a native among natives
but still a stranger
to my skin. I do not
understand a word
when spoken.
I find it hard to walk among

the rolling marbles
but the promise of a perch
fills me with hope.

I FEND OFF WHAT WAS DONE BEFORE

The bread tastes old to me
the more I chew it.
I am a dog with claws
savaging a tree   a vagabond
enamored of his past
& preening.
I can make men's loins
contract. I forecast
darker days. My pleasures
vanish with my hair. I sleep
in thrall recalling times
I clamored for
atonement. I fend off
what was done before
& find it boring.
My fondest wish is for
the pack to tree me.
I camp out in an open field
clean shaven. I gasp
after my belly sags.
I am the master of
a castle where
disaster beckons.
I will be the final hope
of those who cherish
murder.   Cruelty
has never been a crime
for me   nor love
an act of kindness.

I AM NOT LIKE ANYONE AMONG YOU

I feel a sagging
in my legs
I can't stamp out.
Dark as the day becomes
I know no terror.
I play the selfish wolf
beating your doors
until a lintel
splinters.
My blues are in my shoes.
I give my brothers
their own eyes.   (T. U Tam'si)
A spectral witness
I am not like anyone
among you. I lie coiled
while dreaming,
fecund when I rise from sleep.
I trip the light fantastic
—do I not?—
to let my hands break free
from yours.
I take a page from
someone else's
book. My temperature
is equal to
my tidings.
I am twice the man
you courted.
Look at me & see
a gypsy's eyes
in mine. Be fitful.
Find me a place
to sit
& I will repair
the world.

I FEEL THE SAND BETWEEN MY TEETH

Night has the shape of
a wolf's cry.   (A. Pizarnik)
A thimble tapping
on a wash board.
Spoons & castanets.
I feel the sand
between my teeth
my tongue in rapid motion
spit & grit.
I sit under a canvas,
wind & stars
in tune with signals
keyed in dreams.
After I fled from time
the odds turned equal.
I pivoted & fell.
The easy echo of my voice
mingled with theirs.
My lips began to sing
my eyes to scream
past rhyme & reason.
I was a mile ahead
of where the pack ran,
loping like a bear.
I put away my cares & woes
met them as equal
partners. Kitchen politics
proved fatal.
I descended from an ape
& wagged my finger.
There are spooky things
to cope with, worms
to eat, pronounced
gusanos.
I prepared myself
by moonlight
snagged a place among
the rat-faced killers
to redeem my prize.

I VENT MY WRATH ON ANIMALS

I came alive
when things went
crazy.
I pulled the plug on
the reports of
sturm & drang
When someone
signaled I
left open
what I
could not close.
I broke a
covenant that
was more fierce
than murder.
I vent my wrath
on animals
pretending they will turn
divine.
I open up
rare certainties
that test free will.
I take from animals
a place in which
the taste of death
pours from their mouths
& drowns them.
I support a
lesser surface.
I draw comfort from
the knowledge
of their
being.

IN THE WAY WORDS RHYME

In the way words
rhyme
or fail to
I found my truth.
I walked through little parks
elated   crooning.
In the parade of angels
I was first to start.
My life bled through
my skin.
I was connected to the moon
by sonar.
What I couldn't
get a grip on
I discarded.
Sooner than slip back
I let the wranglers
ride me.
I felt my jaw
disgorging
every word
I spoke.
The smell of
mackerel
was the greatest
poem. America was
promises.
I thrust my hand in yours
& yammered.
Miracles came cheap
& fast. I beat myself
with nettles
until the flesh
fell off.
I made a rhyme
of womb
& slaughter,
filling in
the empty sounds.

I ACCEPT THEIR NOMINATION

At night I touch
her mouth
with language.   (D. Meltzer)
She is a trouble shooter
more than me
& answers every call.
I pack a little phone
into my pocket.
I determine to go armed.
A thief's life
beckons. I accept their
nomination &
am instantly in love.
A spokesman for
the desperate
I weep in desperation.
Time assails me.
I defend your household
more than mine.
I shine electric, tingling
when I meet
the grim inspector.
I am the leader of
a band of
goslins. Read me
& instructions
will be clear.
I fight the final
revolution. Peace
draws nigh.
The mark of teeth on flesh
signals our end.

85
FECKLESS WITH DISGUST

All erasure of pain
is like the contrary of
dust that weighs
dark in my lungs
when I am
feckless with disgust.
I stroke & poke
my loins before
they tighten.
My feet stomp
fields of color
reminding me of
something I once knew.
Dying frees
the spirit
from the mind.
We plod along
regardless of
the pain.
Soon we grow
big & fat.
We stop
forgetting, far off
from whatever
binds us
mindlessly
to empty space.
Beginning here
we reignite
desire.
We will surrender
what is far from us
& call it love.

CONFESSIONS

I have confessions
still to make
not least the price
of milk & honey.
I walk through markets,
finger the small
notions, where the language
of my childhood
lingers. Nomenclature
is a form of flattery.
I dwell among you
as your king.
I wear a warning
bloodcoat
& I stand on Elba.   (G. Kouwenaar)
Something wets my face,
the ache of love
perhaps,
the trace of flies in amber.
I bear a hundred names.
I sound them one by one
but none rings true.
For me the urge to plunder
spurs me on. I faint
but laugh myself
awake.
In times less fine
than these
I would have raged.
What's mine
is kept from me.
I drop down on
my knees & kiss
the ground.

BECAUSE COMPLETENESS IS OUR VIRTUE

In spite of suffering
I stand here in
your stead.
I see secret dreams   (P. Neruda)
& shudder.
As cold as light
can be I vie
for lightness.
I count your emeralds
as worthless gauds.
Your fate alarms me.
I am doomed to vanish
in your vanishing.
Understood at last
I smile
because completeness is
our virtue.
I find a message waiting
on my screen.
Our flight departs at noon.
The hole in time
allows my mind
to bridge the darkness.
I marvel at your thoughts
that burst inside me
one by one.
Your loyal servant
not your keeper
I prepare a gathering
where friends,
anxious for sex,
find peace.
I wait with them
until the calendar
runs out, then wear
their empty words
like stars
over my heart.

The voice on the cable
is my own voice
barely heard. The lights
shine bright in Frisco.
From a tower high above
the fabled city
someone sights a gun
& spikes me.
His is a mystery
in a conundrum.
The more I track him
down the more
he skitters.
A stadium of partners
waits on us.
The metal casket
vibrates,
the crystal cracks.
He is no more
a quarterback
than I
a wide receiver.
I plot a life
based on
his resolutions.
Maybe we will meet again
where life is cheap.
I race up stairways
over empty lots
& see myself
backed up against a wall.
I take no prisoners
because the yard
is teeming.
My knuckles on
the table top
I signal twice,

then back away
& leave the meal
uneaten.

A LITTLE THOUGHT

I almost said the bird   (D. Antin)
but meant the word.
Instructions to the police
flew back at me
a great impediment
to public speech.
My doubts were commonplace.
I pounced but did not
bare my claws.
What I would tear off
in a clump
would stay asunder,
a little thought that
filled the world.
Not sanctified
nor wronged
I was their harbinger.
I planned the dreaded evening.
Turmoil on the bridge.
A suit of clothes
minus a body.
I almost said a word
but meant a bird
& ducked it.
I will offer up
no hostages
to fortune.
My right hand
& your left
are linked
in photos   piped
around the globe.
I want my likeness back
because I am not
me without it.
Daft or not
I doze here, waiting
for my flesh

to be interred.
I almost said *absurd*
& meant it.

THE VICTIM I ONCE SHUNNED

My denial of faith
is less than what
the sand laps up
deep in my blood
& leaves me trapped
with my abstractions.
I deactivate
my veins before
they burst.
My neck protrudes
a little more
each summer
less in sleep.
Asphyxiation clears
a pathway
for the soul.
I haul myself
to shore, wet
with despair.
Too late I blossom
& no longer
fearful, far
from anyone who offers
refuge, I am
now the victim I
once shunned.
Rekindled
I exceed
my lust until
it flickers.
I escape the
weight of it
where charity gives way
to greed.

IN FROZEN MOTION

The way my cock itched
when I pissed   (P. Picasso)
made me fretful.
I was barely half awake
enough to follow
where the daydream led me
back to sleep.
The children on the train
were awful. They would bite
& count the time
without a hint of failure.
Eight o'clock was dinner
in the flatlands.
I was what you
might have been
what I was
more than once.
I kicked a stone &
heard the voice
of God.
The pain ran
from my leg
to where
the body splits.
I called my fingers
crucibles.
The soggy smell of dirt,
the open sores,
gave little comfort.
I had kept my steps
abreast of theirs,
then turned &
cantered, closer
to their lights
in frozen motion.

I LET THEM SPEAK FOR ME

The celebrants,
trapped in their gardens,
sink or swim.
It is more than
they can bear
or I can offer them
like pablum on
my fingers.
Now I let them
speak for me
reclaiming roles.
I calculate
& they deliver.
Where their shoes glow
on the stage
a chorus of dark men
beats out a riff.
I walk a mile until
my heart skips
then walk back.
I try to tell them what
they mean but know
their words are mine
not yours or hers.
I play the name game
far from home
where brides are taking photos
in the ruins
schoolboys are beating drums.
I float a whisper
skywards.
Take my picture
when it's dark
& see my aura glow
in blue.
I shine this light for you
over the sleepers.

I WRITE MY NAME ON AIR

I write my name
on air. My tongue
is numb
although it rattles
when I speak.
I dwell among you &
I dish out dreams.
I am a little god
who brays
on impulse.
Do not hesitate to call.
Your smallest wish
is sacred to me.
Sacred too is how
I ride you, spurs
into your sides.
We have no mothers
only cows
no fathers but the wind.
We glide above a painted street
bright houses &
faint smiles. A lady
yanks a comb
out of her hair
& greets us.
Tired from his "show"
a red man
tips his hat.
He grows until
he overflows
the world.
In gratitude
we bow the while
he flaunts his ribbons
gaily.

94
I FAIL AS A CELIBATE

Despair leaves
a dry spot
the passage of light
through my veins.
I fail as a celibate.
The smell of honey
fills my throat.
I lose touch with
my bone when
it stiffens.
Sometimes
I find a place
to spring
& spike you
while you cry.
I try to rev things up
although I hate
the sound of flying.
Gagging leaves
the breath
no exit.
Then the chest puffs out,
no longer hapless,
in the face of
everything aloof
& distant,
where the world begins.
I go on craving
hostile to the ones like you
who bind me.
I surrender any
knowledge of the cave
in which I hide
from light.

I AM THE UNCOMMITTED

Singing in the rain
I felt the earth
tip forward
stranding me
among the thankless
dead.
Magnesium had qualities
like light.
It was the song
that moved me
not the atmospherics
but the strain.
I am the uncommitted
(wrote a friend) *I wear this hero's*
cross   for all my
frowardness   (R. Kelly)
& more. Tacticians
stumble. War is neither
cheap nor timely.
Holocaust or not, I
have a bone to pick
with you, will put my dreams
on hold, to show it.
Left is right to me
& down is up.
I am a heap of
damaged goods, a wreck
like everyone,
nor can I fight it.
I who am distant
even to myself
inch forward to the well.
I bare an arm.
I slash it
eager for the blood
to stain my lips.
The temperatures by day
grow warmer.

There is good reason for alarm.
I switch the television off
& eat my name.

I EXCEED MY LIMITS

I have tried an *altenstil*
& dropped it.
My skin is blazing,
blazing too
the way I see your faces
in the glass.
With the circle of the sun
behind me
I exceed my limits.
My garments are
from the beginning
& my dwelling place
is in my self.   (J. Dee)
It makes me want
to fly   the stars
below   the paradise of poets
lost in space.
I am the father of a lie
unspoken.
I can make my mind
go blank
then paw at you
my fingers in
your mouth.
I think of God
when fucking.
Is it wrong to pray
without a hat
to reject the call
to grace? I long to flatter
presidents & kings.
I long for manna.
I will be the first
to sail for home
the last to flaunt
my longings.
I will undo my garments
& stand before you

naked. In winter
I will curse their god
& die.

97
IN LOVE WITH LOVE

I dreamed,
fingers in my dream.   (Unsi al-Hajj)
A crowd lined up
& cheered me
when I awoke.
I was the happy warrior
a gypsy king
whose minions
dance on water.
In love with love
I shot out threads
to snag the living.
Mud ran from my hands.
I tagged the backs of children
then sprang free.
In summer I became
a tree. In winter
I was hatless.
I saw my face
on a five dollar bill
with glasses.
Gifts were plentiful.
In the way I
made my way
around the rink
I was a winner.
Sure as sin
& distant as
creation
I dropped a button
into space
& heard it thunder.
Boum boum   (T. Tzara)
sang my heart.
My cup ran over.
I never thought of vespers
before I croaked.

A LIVING HEART

I suck on smut
& call it
cuitlacoche.
Lemons open circles
for my eyes.
I can't retreat or wriggle
when the cry of nature
stifles me.
A line of anchovies
streams by.
How bright &
colorful I seem
adorned with
light bulbs
spangled
banging out a riff
in $^3/_4$ time.
Can I love you
even as a devil?
(Can I not?)
The rush of so much
unlived life
leads me to wonder.
What I sniff
is eglantine
the vapors of
which god?
I dine & rest
no closer to the truth
than yesterday.
The table sags
under the burden of
a living heart.
Birds drown in flight.
I make a replica
& stitch it
to my chest.

(G. Sonnevi)

I stare into the god's
eyes & see only
flecks of light.

I AM THE PRESIDENT OF REGULATION

I am the Giant Goliath,
I digest goat cheese.
I am a mammoth's calf.   (H. Ball)
I know your pinnacles by name.
My fingers close around
your fingers. I grow pale.
I become your executioner.
I come forth fat & bloody.
I propose a toast to peace.
I am the president of regulation.
None are savvier than I.
I forge a pact with murderers.
I claw my way to freedom.
Mark my words. I have no time
to be your humble servant.
I make a rope from women's hair.
I bite into the mighty pippin.
I turn & then return by turning.
I turn a vessel over with my hands.
I turn a pretty penny.
I am called the lord of dimes.
I turn my thoughts to daily deeds.
I turn my eyes to heaven.
I turn a screw no one has turned
before me. I predi*cate*
& postposition freely.
In me the numbers come to naught.
I find a secret world in mirrors.
My fingernails are pale,
my steps are perpendicular.
I parachute & strut.
I seek acceleration day by day.
I am a man who swims among the drifters.
Istanbul is not my home.
I turn a page & listen.
I am as hard as nails.
My body swells from all the sounds inside it.
I show myself in dreams.

I am that I am
the god trills.
(He is no more a god
than I or you.)
We see his little boats
ride to the shore
& watch our fathers
like our children
muscle through the waves.
There is a cry
like anybody's
in my throat.
There is a crowd
that fails to see
how our flesh flakes off.
All eyes discern me
where I fall.
No one demands
the tribute
that I cast aside.
I cannot bear it
when they foul my nest.
All that I keep
from those who
sleep beside me
is the calculus of
who they are.
I scorn old people &
discount their days.
I add the numbers
to the newly born
without a thought of
how or why.
I puzzle my old
ways & hide
my fecklessness.
Today is Saturday
forever.

The book is ending
where the book
began.

Postface

A Book of Witness was my passage from one century—one millennium—to another. The first fifty poems were written in 1999, the second fifty in the two years that followed. When I came into the street that first day in the year 2000, it was one of those bright California mornings, & I was struck, very forcefully, by the curious name of the year & by a feeling that I was entering another world. While I didn't put much stock in that kind of era-shifting, my mind that morning still held an image from something I had seen on television the night before—a series of movie clips showing earlier twentieth-century views of what the coming century would be like. *Millennium* was a word I had been mulling over in that closing decade, most notably in the assemblage *Poems for the Millennium* that Pierre Joris & I put together & published in the later 1990s. The word itself, we knew, was slippery—associated as it was with a sense of apocalypse & destruction that often belied our rosier interpretations.

Witness was another word we held in common. In its twentieth-century usage it had a meaning—pathetic but real—that spoke to the horrors, great & small, that marked that time & that persist today. I had come to think of poetry, not always but at its most revealing, as an act of witnessing—by the poet directly or with the poet as a conduit for others. I had also been struck by how crucial to all of that the voice was; I mean the voice in the grammatical sense, the "first person" centered in the pronoun "I." I was aware, even so, of how that first person voice had either been debased or more often despised by many poets—often (where despised) by poets close to me. The intention, understandably enough, was to free the poem from its lyric shackles—"the lyrical interference of the individual as ego," as Olson called it.

The loss of such expression, however, would be immense, & its elimination futile. For there are a number of ways in which that voice—first person—has been one of our great resources in poetry, something that turns up everywhere in our deepest past & present. I mean here a first person that isn't restricted to the usual "confessional" attitude but is the instrument—in language—for all acts of witnessing, the key with which we open up to voices other than our own. I am thinking here of someone like the Mazatec shamaness María Sabina (& her echo in the work of our own Anne Waldman), who throws up a barrage of "I" assertions, when it's really the voices of the gods, the "saint children" of her pantheon, whom she feels speaking through her.

There is in all of this a question of inventing & reinventing identity, of experimenting with the ways in which we can speak or write as "I." In the course of putting that identity into question, I have brought in statements now & again by other poets—very lightly sometimes but as a further way of playing down the merely ego side of "I." And I let the voices that I draw in shift & move around. I want to do that, to keep it in suspense. "I am I because my little dog knows me," Gertrude Stein wrote in a poem she called "Identity." I have written a hundred of these poems now— a century of poems—& I hope that they're both of this time & still connected to the oldest ways in which the poem makes itself.

2001/2002